TRIUMPH HOUSE
Poetry with a Purpose

A PLACE IN MY HEART

Edited by

CHRIS WALTON

First published in Great Britain in 1999 by
TRIUMPH HOUSE
1-2 Wainman Road, Woodston,
Peterborough, PE2 7BU
Telephone (01733) 230749

All Rights Reserved

Copyright Contributors 1998

HB ISBN 1 86161 452 7
SB ISBN 1 86161 457 8

FOREWORD

Love in its many forms touches everybody's lives; whether it is a family pet who has warmed your life or a loved one or close friend from past or present. This anthology of poetry focuses on the theme of love, examining the feelings it evokes in us all.

Poetry has become an extremely popular form of expression over the years, so there is no better way of communication to use to express one's feelings and emotions.

We believe both new and established poets will find this anthology inspiring and will return to it for entertainment and enlightenment for years to come.

Chris Walton
Editor

CONTENTS

Femme Sole	Audrey Anne Sharpe	1
When Love Is Pain	Evelyn Leite	2
Love's Distance	Frederica Morgan-Littleworth	3
The Feeling Of Love	Margaret Fallon	4
Living For Love	Sarah Elizabeth Barker	5
Than You For Everything	Ian Proctor	6
Flower Border	G W Dawson	7
A Sestina For You	Denis Collins	8
Journey Of Discovery	I Williams	10
Love, The Magician	Celia G Thomas	11
Quaint Proposal	Mary G Kane	12
Attraction	Luke Hopkins	13
Intrusion	Patricia McDonald	14
True Love	Janine Dickinson	15
Always Forever	Christine Pledger	16
Love's Tears	Victoria Bern	17
It's Beautiful	Marsha-Lee Barnes	18
To My Love	Eunice C Squire	19
The Egyptian Girl On Crete	Peter Gillott	20
My Love For You	Leann Marie Elkins	21
Every Time	Robert W Moore	22
Together	J M H Barton	23
Love In The Eye	Peter Davies	24
Transfer Your Love	M Rossi	25
Welcome Summer - The Season Of Love	Marjorie Ridley	26
A Natural-Born Beauty	Paul Bartlett	27
There's A Place In My Heart	The Magic Poet	28
I Love	Rachel Ward	29
Gone	Jennifer Tuckett	30
For The Sake Of Friendship	Perry McDaid	31
Love	T Hartley	32
Satellite	Simon G Learman	33
The Golden Time	Elizabeth Mark	34
Petalled Bed	Patricia Campbell-Lyons	35
Unrequited	Elsie Norman	36

Summer Of Love	Leonard T Coleman	37
In Love, Beware The Icons	Ron Hails	38
Thanks For Loving Me	Billy Kennedy	39
Summer Morn	Barbara J Settle	40
A Day To Remember	David Tallach	41
Sand Between My Toes	Anna C Bateson	42
If Life Were Better Yet	Susan Turner	43
Love Span	Di Bagshawe	44
Vision Of Beauty	A Lifeson	45
Love's Tune	Hayley Beddoes	46
Summer Of Love - Chance Encounter	Joan Miles	47
Our Love	K Lake	48
Summer Love	R Griffis	49
Flowers For Mary	Susan Goldsmith	50
Summer Love	Bert Quick	52
Love In Paris	Cynthia Beaumont	53
One Day	Dorothy Pope	54
My Love And I	Rosemary Gill	55
Disputation	George	56
The Dove Of Love Fell Off His Perch And Died	Jan A Krupa	57
I Think Of You	A W Kennedy	58
Jacqueline	Sheila Thompson	59
The Dedicated Fundraiser	Denis Martindale	60
Untitled	Olive Allgood	61
Love, Ode To My Family	Robin Halder	62
Precious Memories - Of Jimmy, Charlotte And Bill	Julie Lambe	63
Untitled	John C Jarratt	64
My Sister Joan	M E Clarke	65
To Albie - RIP	David J Gaywood	66
In Doubt	Winnifred Edith Ross	68
The Love Of Nan	Helen Rowberry	69
Semper Reformanda	Ronald Manley	70
Granny Mac's (An Evocation Of Long Ago)	Verity Gill Malkinson	71
A Blink Of An Eye	David Anton Suessmuth	72

Summer Of Love	Ann Boffey	73
Dedication	Evelyn M Harding	74
Our Times Together	Paul Lowe	75
Send It On Ahead	Keith Johnson	76
Ode To My Sisters	Lachlan Taylor	78
If You Were An Actress	Albert Edwin Fox	79
Broken Love	Kelly Oakley	80
Summer Love	Joy Benford	81
Love	Virginia Withers	82
Is This Really Goodbye	Carolyn Foggin	83
Thoughts	Mary Dimond	84
To My Sister-In-Law	Muriel Schönfield	85
A Life To Lose	Barry Holland	86
Love At First Sight	Brian McDoneli	87
My Summer Love	Margaret Andrews	88
Today I Saw An Angel	Leah Danielle Carey	90
To My Beautiful And Precious Niece, Lauren	'Auntie' Lynn Harper	91
Mother	Marion Warby	92
It Had To Happen	P M Wardle	93
Thoughts Of You	Wendy Watkin	94
Sun On My Face	Zoe Westwood	95
You Gave Me Love	Janet 'Rose' Marsh	96
To My Lover	Marcela Griffiths	97
The Love Of My Life	Laura Keightley	98
Love	Ann Dutschak	99

Femme Sole

When summer dies
I'll cry September tears
And put on Autumn's gaudy mourning
All stark winter hold fast my breath
'Til heaven casts down virgin snow
To blanket white all decay and hush
The chattering hedgerows where shy Spring
Prepares her debut but thirty dawns away
And cautious songbirds trill
Uncertainly at first, then one morning
Suddenly in joyous rapture
Now enter Summer laughing
And the west wind caresses
All her youthful glory
Murmuring 'Only mortals die'
Until again I'll cry September tears.

Audrey Anne Sharpe

WHEN LOVE IS PAIN

It lives in a thousand hearts
the joy of love . . . yet
in a million more, the pain,
in some the agony's intense
helps to destroy;
in some the bond in heaven
is blessed
or does employ
a spirit nobler than the rest.
Are we free to choose
we well may ask
or why the winds of change
blow hot and cold
upon our mask.
As long breathes man
so long love's mystery
will still remain,
the grains of hope die hard
when love's in vain.

Evelyn Leite

LOVE'S DISTANCE

So quietly did you go, untold,
I did not even know,
that never more would arms enfold,
and rapture I'd forego.

But music known far back in time,
Goes on, as in a song,
Recaptured rhythm moves in rhyme,
I know - I still belong.

Frederica Morgan-Littleworth

THE FEELING OF LOVE

These three little words are
   meant for you.
All over the world they are meant
   for them too.

It's a word you can feel,
   but you cannot touch.
Words from the heart you cannot hear.
   Words that mean so much.

This word means a lot,
   but you can't explain.
It makes you happy,
   but also heartbreak and pain.

Little things you do,
   and things that you say
remind me of love
   in a wonderful way.

My thoughts are buzzing,
   and the heart is beating,
now there be no more seeking.

You can't explain
   the way you feel.
I can't I know,
   but I know it for real.

Margaret Fallon

LIVING FOR LOVE

There's a hole in my life that needs to be filled,
And a passion inside that needs to be killed.
There's a spark in my soul that lights to a flame,
And a leap in my heart when you call out my name.
There's an ache in my chest when you're miles away,
And a lump in my throat when you're home to stay.
There's a shiver down my spine when you hold me tight,
And a glint in my eyes when you stay the night.
There's a dream in my mind that's just come true,
And a feeling inside that you love me too.

Sarah Elizabeth Barker

THANK YOU FOR EVERYTHING

Thank you for everything.
For all the love you give.
Without you I'm nothing
And I wouldn't want to live.
I walk with you and talk with you.
I hold your hand in mine.
I bless the day you came my way
Until the end of time.

A walk in the park.
A kiss in the dark.
Our laughter's as young as we are.
Like a couple of kids on a roundabout.
Love is our lucky star.

No matter what they throw at us
Now you are by my side
Our love and faith can conquer all
For you're my strength and guide.
Thank you for Joan and Bob
And for putting up with me.
You're the rock that keeps us all
Together as a family.
But most of all my thanks dear Beth
For always loving me.

Ian Proctor

FLOWER BORDER

Little garden full of flowers
Pink, blue, yellow and white
How bright your colours every year
To give us all delight.

The work we do to keep you straight
With blossoms and green trees
Is work the while so long as you
Continue to bloom and smile.

The border near is both straight and green
Created by tiny plants
A neat and pretty edging piece
Of interest to all who garden
Pyrethrum Linium with leaves so small
Is nature's creation of striped green

The delphiniums are so beautiful
Tall and stately, blue and white
Creations to enhance your plot
A breathtaking summer sight

From June the pretty border glows
With flowers of glorious hue
Centres yellow, velvet wholes
And bells of pink and blue.

G W Dawson

A Sestina For You

I have seen the glorious days of spring
and felt the challenge of the morning sun
that falls across your white and tender skin.
I have touched your lips with a gentle love,
more gentle than the velvet of your eyes,
more gentle still than all your precious dreams.

And this true love could fill your nightly dreams,
with thoughts more clear than any sparkling spring.
'Tis then that I would open up your eyes
and force your stare to dwell upon the sun,
to burn the image of your former love
clean from your heart and from your soft, soft skin.

Remember now the feel of his fair skin
dispel that fondness to the world of dreams,
such memory is but a trick of love
that fools each one of us and then does spring
to torture us under the summer sun
'til we have burning hurt instead of eyes.

Then think you carefully upon my eyes,
recall when I alone could touch your skin
when I alone was your luminous sun.
Were those times real or did you think, 'he dreams
too much, his passion like a coiléd spring
will break and then strike out against my love.'

Is it wrong that I should feel so much, love
so much that I can't look into your eyes
without rage, rage that knows no cooling spring,
that lets no calming air rest on my skin,
knows only the torment of winter dreams,
and the blazing light of the summer sun?

Love me again as you did in the sun,
with all the joy, the anger and the love,
with thirsty cries of passion and with dreams
of life forever; damn his perfect eyes,
bite into my pale flesh and tear my skin,
draw blood and mock the freshness of his spring.

Come into the sun, uncover your eyes,
reject his pallid love and softest skin,
Dream again our dreams, banish him to spring.

Denis Collins

JOURNEY OF DISCOVERY

Pause at this cross-roads.
It's been a long solitude.
No easy route on
this untrodden way.

Others have pondered,
unsure of the territory,
'played safe' by turning
and walking away.

Tread very softly
if you are to venture here:
patience and caution
your passwords must be.

No hasty journey
but, slowly, discovering
different blossoms
upon every tree.

Will it be worth it?
Last chance now, before you start.
No guarantee of
a paradise land.

But, if you're certain
you're travelling this nature trail
then I am humbled
and give you my hand.

I Williams

LOVE, THE MAGICIAN

If I could ride the crescent moon,
I'd harness all its silvery beams,
So moonbows, shining through the rain,
Would bathe you in translucent streams.

If I could mount the Milky Way,
I'd pocket all the creamy stars,
Then shower constellations bright
To hear you sound your loud hurrahs.

If I could scale the rainbow's arc
To steal its colours from the skies,
I'd take the gold to gild your hair
And violet to tint your eyes.

If I could rein the racing winds,
I'd tame them with an expert hand.
Only zephyrs would cool your brow -
Only to come at my command.

If I could change the season's clocks
So flowers would bloom before they should,
And leaves would grow on winter trees,
But only in our magic wood,

Then in December you could walk
Through woodland green with foliage,
Where buds would have a second spring,
And rocks would sprout with saxifrage.

If I could rule the elements,
Would I have power over you,
And if I did, would you respond
With loving kindness deep and true?

Celia G Thomas

QUAINT PROPOSAL

We strolled among the heather on a Sunday afternoon,
My love and I together, the month was flaming June,
We kissed, he popped the question, 'Will you
marry me?' he said. 'I will' said I
'But still you'll have to go and ask my dad.'

My dad was none too happy when he asked him
for my hand, 'Take all of her or nothing'
Was my father's curt command
'I've kept her long enough now it's someone else's turn
But if you want to marry her
Some lessons you must learn.'

He looked him over, summed him up
And grunted 'Hmm, not bad!' and added as an
Afterthought, 'he seems a likely lad.'

With crushing condescension Father said,
'She could do worse,
But just make sure my daughter
has some money in her purse.

He gave a grudging blessing with a
binding stipulation, he said
'You must provide for her?' and
'What's your occupation?'

'Just make sure you keep her in
the style she's in today,
If you make this promise then I'll
give you my OK.'

So now we're wed I'm housed and fed,
Dad couldn't be more pleased,
At last I'm off his hands and
his financial burdens eased.

Mary G Kane

ATTRACTION

We are falling through space together
but have barely a notion
of the speed of our motion
since gravity keeps things
from falling apart

We are falling in love together
spinning and streaming
waking not dreaming
through quantum leaps
of strangeness and charm

We are travelling through time together
through curved space and dark matter
hurtling toward the Great Attractor
with our senses reeling
with our minds peeling
with our hearts healing
with the earth receding
approaching the vanishing point
of escape velocity and critical mass.

Luke Hopkins

INTRUSION

Intrusive iceberg
Penetrating my emotions
Ripping trust asunder
Frantically.
Icy boulders of destruction
Submerging, sinking
Love - dying, engulfed
Titanically.

Patricia McDonald

TRUE LOVE

Play another song . . . my tears need to fall
My heart needs to remember that summer call
Sing the words that were yours and mine
The music can let the mind re-live our time
Read the poems I wrote for you
Let your heart release a tear or two
Look at the pictures and what's inside
Remember a secret love we had to hide?
Have all your memories drifted afar
Wishes I sent to you by a star
Can you remember? Relax your mind
Our times are there for you to find
An inspiration you were to me
The spirit inside that you set free
Dedications! Have they gone?
Remind my heart play me another song
Mime the words take away my pain
Find that feeling once again
That summer sun that shone each day
Dreams that came true don't let them fade away
A broken heart can never forget
The love and happiness ended with regret
Whispered words our hearts said each night
We had the love to hold us tight
I never thought it would be like this
You're the only one I miss
Shane is the name that makes me cry
Although it's the strength that gets me by
Forever will be kind if you're with me
I've learnt now that's the way we'll always be.

Janine Dickinson

Always Forever

I lie in bed awake at night
Thinking of your charms;
But, honestly, I want to be
Enveloped in your arms.

My thoughts of you are always sweet,
I really need no other.
If you were here this minute
With my kisses, I'd you smother.

Do you think I'd leave you?
The answer's never, never!
My love is now for you alone
Always and forever.

Christine Pledger

LOVE'S TEARS

When snow lays soft where grass was green
and golden leaves fall from the trees,
when buds awake to welcome spring.
Come back to me.

When sunset's beauty takes our breath
and Summer warms the coldest day,
when twinkling stars gaze from above.
Come back to me.

When smiles won't reach my tear-filled eyes
and tunes of love bring thoughts of you,
when memories sear my aching heart.
Come back to me.

Victoria Bern

It's Beautiful

I blinked and there I was in my secret garden,
time to do what I love . . .
I waltzed and tangoed with the silver sea - feeling ripples of joy.
I shook hands with the sun, it felt hot and receptive. It smiled a blanket
of love.
Then I drew pictures of babies in the clouds
Feathers of warmth brushed against my skin.
Anything's possible in my secret garden.
I played mind games with the wind, he tossed and turned me,
I didn't stand a chance so I made a truce.
Then relaxed in beds of soft cotton while the seagulls sang to me . . .
'He loves you, he loves you, how sweet it is!'

Marsha-Lee Barnes

To My Love

The night is dark, the moon is clouded o'er,
Waves of the sea roll up on the shore,
White billowy foam covers pebbles so small
And God above is over all.

No boats do I see, nor children small,
And no buckets and spades up on the wall
No seagulls I see, soaring up high,
Yet still I feel my Father nigh.

There is not even a deckchair in sight,
But all is so calm in the pale moonlight.
The silvery fish swim beneath the sea,
It's all so wonderful to me.

The stars are hid, but now the moon is out
And we are so free just to walk about,
We are just on our own, my man and I,
Walking beneath a moonlit sky.

We're hand in hand, gaily tripping along,
Down in our hearts, love's old sweet song,
As we have done now for many a year,
Our Lord beside us, ever near.

But our evening stroll must come to an end
As we drive homeward, round the bend,
Through dark hills, and through leafy lane
Until we reach our home again.

Eunice C Squire

The Egyptian Girl On Crete

The Egyptian girl is hitching from beach to beach.
Such a handsome face. Wrinkled black hair. A miracle
of emancipation, she assaults bare-legged each conservative hamlet.

Old women scowl behind distaffs but their grandsons
tighten a noose of chairs around this elusive goddess
in a cool bar betrayed by crates of fizz bottles.
They do not touch. They adore at close quarters.
'What is your name?' 'Where are you from?'
'My name is Charmian. I am Egyptian but I live in Paris.'
'You are beautiful. Will you marry me?'

Her companion Jacqueline sulks in accustomed isolation.

At sunset Charmian wades the clean sands of Falasarna,
scrutinised by Germans from tent and cavern.
'Are you alone?' 'My friend is coming.'
'You sleep here?' 'We're camping.' 'Where?' 'I don't remember.'

At sunrise she swims naked near the sign: *No Nudism.*
She dries herself slowly. The breeze snatches her towel
concealing, revealing brown breast and thigh.
The landworker, who kissed the priest's hand
watches furtively, concealed by an olive tree.
The vision of her body will torment him nightly.
He will ravish her though she is a thousand miles distant.

Already she is leaving. 'We are flying to Geneva.
Oh! I have a thorn in my foot.' But it is Jacqueline who winces,
presuming another artifice to gain attention.

I buy them drinks in the village. Jacqueline says, 'Thank you.'
But Charmian is bullying a cowed truck-driver.
'Take us to Khania. Alright then. Kastelli.'
She mounts the truck. She stands like a commander.

I am abandoned with the wounded in the dust of her chariot.

Peter Gillott

My Love For You

You mean the world to me
I just wanted you to know
I love to hold you close
and never let you go
I treasure every moment
that we have to share
even in the silence
it's good to know you're there
In the good and the bad
you always show you care.
Just the thought of life without you
I don't think I could bear.
Your tenderness
your warm embrace
the knowledge of your love for me
just warms my heart and makes it race
and so I just wanted to say
I love you more in every way
each and every single day.

Leann Marie Elkins

EVERY TIME

Every time I pass this way
My love, I long to hear you say
I love you dear with all my heart
I love you with a love that's true
I'll spend my whole life loving you
To show you just how much I care
How much you mean to me
As long as I know, that you're there
Whate'er our future has to be
To share our life with time to spare
Just for each other's happiness
To give such joy and heavenly bliss
To hold you in my arms, and say
I love you, every time we kiss.

Robert W Moore

TOGETHER

When unveiled our hearts to those we love
May good fortune attend, perchance to love
Without default, allow your aching heart be healed
Endowed within your beauty, grace revealed.

For a heart, a soul, without deception, plain
Through love's almighty vastness, life regain
Without intrigue corrupt, to you love brought,
Love of another without search, or sought.

For the voice of my heart would simple ask
Your hand in mine, your heart to clasp;
A hand which knows how to comfort much,
A hand so gentle, blessed its touch.

What other for me, but like an empty chalice bring,
A vessel not of love, with dried and empty ring;
But of warmth, joy, compassion, a holy sense to be
Would only right, the one be you for me.

J M H Barton

LOVE IN THE EYE

What - me and Mabel?
Don't be absurd!
Me go out with that atrocious bird!
The one with braces on her gums?
The one that used to help me with my sums?
The freckled one
Who wears a bun?
The one who has a toothy grin,
Who has a pointed chin?
The one who has a sexy look,
Whose head is always in a book?
The one with rounded hips,
Small ears, bright eyes, red lips?
Who's sort of feminine
With silky skin?
What me and Mabel?
What a slur!
I've hardly even noticed her!

Peter Davies

TRANSFER YOUR LOVE

When you've lost your mother or dad,
transfer the love you've had.
So many people out there with nobody
to care.
Weep no more.
Old folks, young people with no homes.
Show them they're not alone.
Empty hole left in your heart
will fill again.
Weep no more.
Become a part of another person's
empty heart.

M Rossi

WELCOME SUMMER - THE SEASON OF LOVE

Summer has arrived it's the season of love
Love is God's special gift - sent from above.
So clap your hands and raise a cheer
The season of love - summer is once again here.

Lovers can be seen strolling hand in hand in the park
Waiting for night to come to make love in the dark
Love is seen in a smile or just a glance
Eyes full of love that say 'Will you take a chance?'

We show our love in so many ways
Love will always be here till the end of our days.
A hug and a kiss can mean so much
But how we all love that special touch.

Summer love is the best of all
The season of love, so let's have a ball.

Marjorie Ridley

A Natural-Born Beauty

How must it be,
To be,
Such a natural-born beauty -

Where a flash
Of a lash,
Causes a good rush of blood
That's good -

While dating
A doting
'Enemy',
That's perpetually bound to see -

A magnificent streamlined galleon,
Parting all waves before her,
Leading her prancing, chancing, stallion,
And vast assembly that adore her,
Forever beckoning 'a battalion' -

Incapable of resisting
Special honour of assisting,
(Impossible to deny her)
In all she would desire -
                    To aspire . . .

Paul Bartlett

THERE'S A PLACE IN MY HEART

Roses are red
Violets are blue
There's a place in my heart
That's reserved just for you

Please will you fill it
As soon as you can
For you are a woman
And I am a man

The blue of your eyes
The red of your lips
The rose of your cheeks
Are at my fingertips

When will you respond
To the way that I feel?
Prove to me that
Our emotions are real?

That is my dream
Please make it come true
In the garden of love
I am waiting for you.

The Magic Poet

I Love

The red flower that blossoms inside me
a bright light shines through the lonely hall
the sense of heat that strikes within me
the nightingale sings with a loving call.
A loving sunset closes the heated day
words cannot justify the thoughts one feels
the perfect timing will come and I will lay
a broken heart in time can tell and heal.
Stars sparkle in the dim loved moonlight
rely on me, and with my strength I will hold
romance opens in the darkness of the night
the flower falls and dies, I am left cold.

Take time in love, be wise and see the light.
Let thee stand beside, and support with bright.

Rachel Ward

GONE

If I go now, will you miss me?
When will you notice that I've gone?
When the first rays of the sun
play on your forehead
and you turn to kiss me
and I've gone.

If I go now, will you miss me?
When you read my letter will the tears
roll down your cheeks for all the years
and the things
you should have done?

If I go now, you will miss me?
For the night is still too young
and our time has not begun
yet you never said the words
and you only tried to kiss me
on the day that I was gone.

Jennifer Tuckett

FOR THE SAKE OF FRIENDSHIP

I know a man of dubious grace,
much over-conscious of his face -
what he sees is to his liking
for none, he swears, be quite so striking.

Blustering, he sips at golden 'jar',
glued to the counter of the bar,
brags of deeds and conquests long gone -
when life was not evening but dawn.

He boasts of his great intelligence,
defames those who'd commit pretence
cloaking gifts with 'false' modesty -
he prefers arrogant *honesty!*

And in *my* wisdom - I patronise
with concurring tongue, scornful eyes -
wond'ring which rates more derision:
My silence . . . or his faulty vision!

Perry McDaid

LOVE

To love someone
Is a special gift
A gift from God
A gift that can lift
Your feelings high
Putting you on a cloud in the sky
It gives so much happiness
To one and all
We all should try it
Don't deny it
It is something we shouldn't ignore
So love, let love, and do it more and more!

T Hartley

SATELLITE

Like Venus, a distant planet,
I am a moon in her orbit,
following a path, forever never ending.
In her aura, through part of her day,
sometimes cloaked in darkness.
Passing close by, never touching,
time and space, keep us distant,
I am the satellite in her mornings' dawn.

Simon G Learman

THE GOLDEN TIME

Midsummer's Eve. This night, I sit with you
Beneath a gentle sky of gold and blue,
In your garden haven. Downs and sea
Encircle us. Such peace. Tranquillity.

My darling, was it really only days
Since we met inside that magic maze?
Both lost and looking for the hidden 'out'.
You found it first. 'This way!' I heard you shout.

You came towards me, stretching out a hand.
Led me to the narrow exit and
Then walked me to the station. 'Ring me, please.'
You begged. I would. I'd never known such ease

Of conversation, laughter, feelings shared.
We talked of things I never would have dared
Discuss with strangers. Being 'lost' for years.
You, too! Deep in that voice were unshed tears.

I felt I *knew* you. Felt you were the brother
I'd never had, but longed for. (Though my mother
Complained that just *one* child had cost her dear.
Put a full stop to her film career!)

 Midsummer's Eve. You offer me a ring
 As golden as the sky, a truly many-splendour thing.
 The love we've forged tonight, no soul can ever prise apart.
 Never more need we endure the winter of the heart.

Elizabeth Mark

PETALLED BED

I awoke and found you sleeping
within my petalled bed,
the stigma of humanity
from toe, to snow-white head.
Materialised from mists of dreams
and unseen bonds that bind,
from quotients of infinity
so strangely undefined.

The scent of splendour
love and time
perfumed and fragrant leaves,
enchanting, subtle, nectar sweet
as honey to the bee,
the ghosts of seasons past and gone,
but they belonged to me.

Patricia Campbell-Lyons

UNREQUITED

I was alone, my spirit wrapped in night
While all around me summer blazed its light.
A flower-filled garden with its colours bright
Alive with living things that mocked my plight!

I was alone. Alone you waited too,
While organ played a melody you knew
And all your dearest crowded every pew:
All waiting for a bride who loved you too.

I was alone: yet swear I heard aright
The change of tempo - there she walked in white!
The gasps of admiration at the sight,
The surge of joyous love those hearts excite.

I was alone. No single thought I drew
Into your mind though all my thoughts of you,
Knowing it closed a dream that sweeter grew
Viewed from afar; that closer I might rue.

Elsie Norman

SUMMER OF LOVE

A boy and girl in love, and holding hands,
To complement a perfect summer day
A scene repeated many times - a wonder,
Which never fails to steal our hearts away.

For all the world is said to love a lover
With eyes that shine, and lips that wear a smile,
Bringing together with a chosen partner
A passionate affair that is worthwhile.

To live their lives together, caring, loving,
Oblivious of time, or age, or even race,
Knowing that they have solved life's great conundrum,
Sharing their friendship with a simple grace.

What can surpass such longing for each other
The dreams, the hopes that make their union one,
To travel on life's stormy road together
Through all its many shades - into the sun.

Leonard T Coleman

IN LOVE, BEWARE THE ICONS

Come, let me remind you
of the timeless tracks of love that led us hence,
when we believed existed, in realms
beyond recall, a sylvan world of quiet reflection;
clamour and boom did not intrude;
the days were spent together;
not, as now, in cyclic genre,
the rhythms of our lives divide.

But, since the mystic path has led us to the present,
let us not destroy the tributes we exchanged:
> the vested words;
> the promises declared;
> the values we espoused.

Around us there abound the opiates of sight and sound,
for our amusement, we believe!

But let these not deceive, or spawn reality from fancy.
For thus, the icons we create, destroy and leave regret,
trampled with the blossoms are the innocents of trust,
whose shattered peace and sundered love,
no time, no words, assuage or heal.

Ron Hails

THANKS FOR LOVING ME

You beautiful person
you would blush if I gave you praise
so I wait until you sleep
then I softly say . . . thank you.

> Thank you baby, for loving me
> loving me with all my faults.
> Thank you baby for devotion
> every storm you are my port.
> Thank you baby, for choosing me
> when other boys wanted you.
> Thank you babe for staying faithful
> when all around are untrue.

I know, it will last forever
this love we share, you and I.
And I know, we will be together
long after the sun has left the sky.

> Baby not once, did you turn away
> the thousand times I looked a mess.
> Thanks for loving me for what I am
> and not the fashion of my dress . . .

Thank you baby, for loving me.

Billy Kennedy

Summer Morn

Awake to a gold-filled morn, my love
Brush silent sleep from thine eyes,
Come forth from thy scented bed, my love
And greet the proud sunrise.

The hazy glow of shimmering dawn
Spreads slow across hill and plain,
And I am waiting, this summer morn
To take thine hand again.

To take it and wander through dewy vale,
And step o'er grassy lea,
Where star-white daisies a pathway make
To welcome thee and me.

O what rapturous song the blackbird trills,
As if by his tender throat
He fain would summon the purple hills,
To list to his perfect note.

And O, my love, the day is fair,
With murmurs and whispering dreams
And I watch the gleam of thy golden hair,
And the silver fish in the streams.

O come let us stay, let us play, my love
While the day is bright and free,
And I'll tell the warm wind of my love, my love
And she'll bring it back to thee.

Barbara J Settle

A Day To Remember
(To Ian And Gillian, with warmest love)

Always to be remembered with fondness,
This flower fragrant day.
Glossy photos of the time will fade,
But their lives together will remain fresh.

First comes the tender sobriety of the church service,
The calmly assertive 'I wills'.
Austere bridegroom black and sparkling bridal white
Joined in hands and lips and hearts.

Friends and relatives have gathered,
Tucked securely in the curving wood-panelled pews,
In smiling solidarity
To applaud the couple's commitment.

I am proud to be cousin to this man,
Taking this woman to be his lawful wedded wife.
From altar vows to altar call
Their priorities are assured from the start.

The long white cloth of the reception's top table
Is a contrast to Ian's familiar stainless steel.
Here the actors of the drama
Perform on a stage of a different theatre.

So many lovely, laughing people,
Shaking with mirth and the rhythm of the dance,
Colourful clan tartans rippling
On the warm summer day, the blue sky bright.

Today seals the convenant of a real and lasting promise,
Never to leave one another, till death us do part.
So many abandon this solid old road,
But these two will never.

David Tallach

SAND BETWEEN MY TOES

There's waves in the caves,
The young girl cried,
With gay abandonment and a pixie's grin.
Like a shrill pup, always bounding and yapping.
But I don't like sand between my toes she wailed!
And sulked and huffed and puffed and cried
Oceans from her eyes.
Her storm cloud face made her father smile,
As he lifted the little sea urchin lightly onto his broad shoulders,
Chuckling all the while.
The little lips pouted,
Are you laughing at me? she demanded,
Her quavering voice high and indignant.
No, no.
At what then?
The clams and quails, sea slugs and snails.
She laughed as she rode him, like a surfer on the waves.

Anna C Bateson

If Life Were Better Yet

It hurts me leaving you so soon
but a new life I must seek,
I couldn't face the future here
in case our love grew weak.

I must go now, my heart is strong,
I have the will to go,
and mustn't leave it lingering long
to wish it were not so.

Then I'll recall a fleeting love
enriching with its joy,
too short for time to weaken
or familiarity destroy.

Or will I find in years to come
my present strength desert me,
and wish I'd stayed to love you more,
or would that too, have hurt me?

It's hard to leave what is so good
and know I may regret;
it would surely be a miracle
if life were better yet?

Susan Turner

LOVE SPAN

When first we met your hair was dark,
And you stood straight and tall,
Cupid's arrow met its mark
We had no doubts at all.
Soon we watched the family grow,
Made for each parental plan -
Anxious when at last they flew
Their new horizons scan.
Slowly our hectic life calmed down,
And we must look within,
Preparing for our own sundown,
Watch the world more gently spin.
In turn our bodies gave a sign
We should not push so hard,
Our life took on a new design,
But our love has not been scarred.
When first we met your hair was dark,
And you stood straight and tall,
Yes! Cupid's arrow hit its mark -
For now I love you most of all.

Di Bagshawe

VISION OF BEAUTY

She was here in the daytime,
And gone in the night . . .
I think that I loved her,
Oh! I loved her all right.
Her face was a picture,
Her eyes shone like stars,
She was close in the daylight,
But now she's so far.

We met in the summer,
With the sky deepest-blue . . .
I think that she loved me,
Oh! she loved me it's true.
So now in the night-time,
I long for the day . . .
Where she will be waiting,
But never to stay.

A Lifeson

LOVE'S TUNE

I know that I never believed in love.
I know that I would never fall so deep.
But you, you proved me wrong.
I never thought I'd know the song
But you, you told me the words
And now I know so much.
I know that I need to be close to you,
Never far away from you.
To carry on one day, one week, one lifetime.
You are my soul and my only love.
You take a breath for you for me.
Without you I'm gone.
But I, I thought it too soon.
But then you went and taught me the tune.
You sang that you loved me,
And now we're in harmony.
One day, one day more may be too late.
I'm stretching out my arms to you,
Reach back and say you love me too.
Before we're gone and hate's won.

Hayley Beddoes

SUMMER OF LOVE - CHANCE ENCOUNTER

I was feeling sad and alone,
When you glanced and smiled at me,
In a kind gentle tone
Your arm you offered me,
I took it with pride,
And walked by your side,
In Washington's town side;
We dined together each night,
You held my hand so tight,
When you kissed me goodbye,
Thinking of you I can but sigh,
Remembering those happy days,
Before we went our different ways;
Maybe we'll meet again one day
And find love has come to stay!

Joan Miles

OUR LOVE

Our love goes back
a long way
to when the world was young
so how can you now say
that for you
them stars have lost their magic spell.
For in another lifetime
love was forever ours
I used to send you flowers.
I still remember it so well.
There was a time
we carved our names within two
love hearts deep into the wood
of the tree
where as children we once stood.
These days the tree still stands
where other lovers now wait
to watch for falling stars
across the night
that shape their fate.
Lovers still holding hands
as they make their future plans
then just wait.

K Lake

SUMMER LOVE

When summer came in full attire
with lark upon the wing,
when sweet maidens brought desire
to make his world a joyous thing.

Sounds of carnival filled the air
to dance and sing was his mean.
Away from carousels' noisy blare,
he found the love to fill his dream.

Dark clouds of war hovered high
and trumpets called to fight
he left his love to take the sky
and fulfil his conscience right.

Long years passed by far from love,
but ever mindful of his care,
till the dove of peace from above
brought him home on wings of prayer.

To love and be loved and to share
in spring he, wed in Christian mould
the love seed brought a daughter fair
to have, to cherish, and behold.

One cold December came a boy
his family to complete.
No words could tell of the joy, that
ever in his heart would beat.

The autumn of his years came on
whence dark sorrow crossed his way
to wake and find his daughter gone
but to leave a summer's love in sweet array.

R Griffis

Flowers For Mary

In a chest full of memories
For Mary I did peep
Searching for the flower
For her hair I did keep
In a tissue parcel wrapped with ribbons bright
Was a gown that held many memories
As it was unfolded this night
My fingers caress the velvet
Through them I let it slip
Uttered words would not come
They were stayed upon my lips
Through the mist of time and tears
I was re-living that night
Long since was the years
Feeling like a queen
As he walked through the door
Extending a gentle hand
We both took to the floor
How the skirt glittered
It shone in the light
Swirling and swaying
Till the stars left the night
A smile on my face as I remember before
Tender hands that had loved me
Now love me no more
Mary so kindly touches my sleeve
Bringing my thoughts back
As she whispers may I please

Standing before me a beauty so fair
In a gown of gold and velvet
With long silken hair
With his hands soft and gentle
He slowly extends
I watch and pray dearly
That their love never ends.

Susan Goldsmith

Summer Love

My summer love, my one and only,
Came to me when I was lonely;
  I can't forget her.
Walked with me and held my hand;
Shared my wandering on the sand
  The year I met her.
Remembering now the place I waited,
Recall the times when we had dated.
  She filled my dreams;
Would buy her flowers though not wealthy,
Cycled miles which kept us healthy,
  Shared my schemes.
We, so young, desired to marry,
Outside bridal shops would tarry
  Making plans to get engaged;
Asking parents for approval
Requested promptly my removal,
  Both enraged!
In December's wind and rain
Took a Northward trip by train
  Up to Gretna Green instead;
Never one to let the grass grow,
Could have gone straight on to Glasgow,
  To get wed.
She at sixteen, me at nineteen,
  Shared a bed.
Nigh on forty years have passed
Since summer love first graced my life;
Winters seem to lose their harshness
In the warmth that she affords, my wife.

Bert Quick

LOVE IN PARIS

Hand in hand we stroll along
Summer boulevards,
Bright July's song
To people.
Cheek to cheek we cuddle
Close together,
And drink a toast
To love.
Knee against knee we sit
Close to each other,
Enveloped by love
In Paris.
Side by side we wander on
Content in the crowds,
Day is gone,
Night reigns.

Cynthia Beaumont

ONE DAY

He showed her rhododendrons,
Hundreds, ruby, pink and purple,
Blooming under giant trees
In dappled sunlight, earthed in red-brown
Beech-mast, inches deep and undisturbed.

The afternoon was hushed and still.
An unintrusive cuckoo merely
Emphasised the forest peace.
No other creatures stirred except
One speculating squirrel and
A startled thrush. A pair of mated
Mallards nestled quietly.

Later on, the couple's bed
Was hung with rhododendrons and
The dim light on the landing cast
A beech-wood shade.

Dorothy Pope

My Love And I

As we walked with arms entwined,
My love and I passed by.
A house very neat and trim
We both remarked with a grin,
'It would be nice to be asked in.'
The years rolled by, each of us getting older,
We had our ups and downs
But they passed over.
My love helping in unseen ways
To brighten our reclining days.
Had we but thought on that bright day,
My love and I would come to stay
In that house so neat and trim
Where all who call will be welcomed in.

Rosemary Gill

Disputation

With a mirage of delight you bought me
You came to me as pale and shifting sand
My thoughts were all of you, and meant to be
With love I fawned the softness of your hand

Your touch was joy, your voice was my command
Beware the trick that takes this well worn track
Too high a price to pay within this strand
The pain inside would dwarf a stretching rack

As many arrows pierce the heart to sack
So, only those who know would know the fear
Who draws the dagger now to stab the back
With words that tumble out upon the ear

  And yet if chance would come to me again
  I'd take my fill for sunshine and for rain.

George

THE DOVE OF LOVE FELL OFF HIS PERCH AND DIED
(for Jude)

The journey seemed a long one
until I looked into the sky, and
wondered if an angel would help
me make the world go by.

So on I gently trod, to a
classified destination, when it
grew and grew upon me, that
this angel was already at every station.

When you look, I see you know,
the wondrous freedom that makes
you go; to the land you love: the land
you know and find a scented blossom.

The wall of purple passes by,
and finds another seated cry,
you see the journey is now too
short,
because angels without wings sometimes
have to fly

Jan A Krupa

I Think Of You

I think of you,
And a smile creeps across my face,
My mind starts to drift away,
My thoughts in outer-space.
I only hear the music,
As we dance arm in arm
Embracing each other -
Free from all harm,
Your hair against my face,
Your warm chest against mine,
As we sway to the music,
Forgetting about time.
Each other exploring,
Roaming hands on the dance floor,
It's time we were leaving,
For I'd like to do more.
Then I wake with a blush,
As my colleague gives a shout,
I've been thinking of you again,
Of that there's no doubt.
I'll see you again,
When I next think of you,
Then we can do all the things,
That our bodies long to do.

A W Kennedy

JACQUELINE
(Dedicated to a Devoted and Loving Daughter)

I'd like to say, a big thank you Dear God,
For my daughter Jacqueline,
I am sure if she entered a competition for the best,
She would easily win!
Now I have reached retirement,
I look back over the years,
She gave me a great deal of happiness,
And never a moment's tears!
Ever thoughtful, ever kind,
Thoughts of her I bring to mind,
She is hardworking as a teacher and a mother,
Jackie deserves the highest praises,
Unlike any other
I like to send her flowers
I hope to bring a smile,
And to show her from my heart,
That I like her style.

Sheila Thompson

THE DEDICATED FUNDRAISER

In every town across the land
We find him holding out his hand -
Collecting funds for charity
From folks like you . . . and folks like me!
He stands there waiting, rain or shine,
Hoping we will not decline
The needs of those that he holds dear -
For whom he chose to volunteer!
They may be starving refugees!
His conscience hears their earnest pleas!
They may be blind, deaf, dumb or lame!
Their plight is now his sacred aim!
They may be helpless, quite forlorn!
A noble cause has just been born . . .
A flood or earthquake, who can say?
And yet, through him, help's on its way!
But only if he stands and waits,
Upon the Council's licenced dates,
For many seek to raise funds, too . . .
From folks like me . . . and folks like you!
It's up to us to contribute -
To play the saint or stay the brute!
Donate a pound or walk on by,
Not asking who or what or why . . .
He simply stands in silent hope
To save some lives . . . help victims cope . . .
So, think again! Don't hurry past!
This chance to help may be the last!
It's up to us to show we care . . .
Just like the man who's standing there . . .

Denis Martindale

UNTITLED

I remember the sound of their marching feet
As I stood with others in the street
It was the boys who were called-up for the war
I had never known anything like this before
Bravely they went to fight the foe
What would they encounter we did not know
Like them I was young that summer day
Not thinking about the price we would pay
How many came back I do not know
They were so brave so willing - ready to go
When I wear my poppy in the street
I can always remember those marching feet.

Olive Allgood

LOVE, ODE TO MY FAMILY
(To my father, mother, Rima, Natasha, Rotna, Bidhan, Sapna, Sunil, all my relatives and in-laws)

Love is a multi-faceted mistress,
Tuning our heartstrings through a myriad of frequencies.
For example, the affection that binds us to our parents who nuture,
Elevate and succour us to the point of adulthood,
Is an unbreakable, eternal staff that knows no description.
This differs from a fraternal attachment when we know that we can
                      receive a pillar of support when times dictate,
Through to the fondness that a sisterly touch brings reminding us of the
            pleasant things in life such as anniversaries and birthdays.
Tenderness is the credo of love when describing filial attachment,
The fact that our sons and daughters are innocent, dependent, creative clay,
That we can mould for the first two decades,
        who express warmth and delight in their ursine embraces,
Perpetuating our own immortality via their very existence!
Passion, is the face of love, when addressed to your wife or partner,
Who will be the creator of future generations,
Which changes to amiable companionship as we both journey through
                             the minefield of life.
Adoration, is the aspect of love, which applies to our grandparents,
                                  uncles and aunts,
Whose regaling tales told in our youth span decades.
Benevolence, amity, dispassion or hatred are the shades of love
                        associated with you in-laws,
Depending on your personal interaction with each!
Like a sparkling diamond's many faces,
Love, means many things to many people depending on its bond!

Robin Halder

PRECIOUS MEMORIES - OF JIMMY, CHARLOTTE AND BILL

My child is gone
And I don't think I can go on
I think of those lovely precious years
Now they're sprinkled with my tears
But somewhere
Through the pain
The precious hope remains
My child is safe
My child's with you
And nothing can ever harm my child again
Lord, you know how I feel
You know my pain
You know this ache in my heart is real
Someday I'll understand
Someday I'll know
Until then Lord
Hold me tight and don't let go.
Thank you Lord
For giving my child to me
And thank you Lord
For all my precious memories.

Julie Lambe

Untitled

To me the best day of my life
Was when dear Mary became my wife
The second day of September
Is a day I shall always remember
The year was nineteen thirty-nine
To us 'everything' seemed fine
But on the next day of that year
War was declared, bringing many a tear
All our plans just went astray
On this third and awful day
But our love did not falter
We said we would not alter
For we all will do our best
To win through, this awful test
This we did from day to day
And at last we found a way
To win through, just once again
This war cost lives, and awful pain
And at last the war was 'won'
To the joy of everyone.

John C Jarratt

My Sister Joan

When I was a child she was there
When I grew up she was there
She was the rock I leaned upon
Someone I always depended on,
She shared all my fears, would dry-up my tears
And stay with me till they were gone.

When it came time to have lives of our own
We were still very close although we were grown,
I'll never forget when she left how I missed her
She'll always be my beloved sister.

Now she helps others with caring and love
She tends the sick with help from above
Everyone loves her, she has so much to give
She has healing powers, so long may she live.

M E Clarke

To Albie - R I P

Albie was a little cat
He hadn't long been born.
He went to see the vet
To have his tummy shorn.

The vet did things inside him,
But he never felt no pain.
He just felt something missing
When he got home again.

Dressed in his brand-new collar,
Though it felt a little tight.
He brushed-up all his whiskers
And went out for the night.

He soon fell into the company
Of a female cat called Fred.
He said, 'You're such a pretty thing
Shouldn't you be home in bed?'

'And who wants to be there with me?'
Her face all wreathed in smiles,
Said she, 'I'm happy here thank you
Walking on the tiles.'

'Oh,' Albie said, 'I'm harmless,'
And explained the situation.
But she didn't quite believe him,
About his operation.

'That's an old, old story,' said she,
'Told by every male
To have their wicked way with us.'
And she flicked him with her tail.

Poor Albie who had never had
And it looked like he never would.
Took his leave of this teasing feline,
And went home in an awful mood!

David J Gaywood

IN DOUBT

(With Love to my Husband Bert. Whom I married when I was sixteen, forty-eight years ago)

I wonder if it's all too late
As I go to meet my fate.
For I am walking down the aisle
When I could really run a mile.

Now I know just what nerves are
And that altar seems so far
But I'll arrive at it in style
And face my future with a smile.

They have booked the horse and carriage
I must go through with this marriage.
And not let on to Mum and Dad
About the change of mind I've had.
For to stop it now I'm guessing
Wouldn't meet with the vicar's blessing.

Still to come that honeymoon.
Oh, I hope it's over soon
And we can turn again to normal
By becoming much more formal

Now my husband, he's so very kind
That being married I don't mind
And wonder what it was all about
That I should be in so much doubt
For now I'm glad I did not falter
On my way up to the altar.

Winnifred Edith Ross

The Love Of Nan
(All our love from the Grandchildren, Great Grandchildren and Great, Great Grandchildren)

She sits in her armchair with a smile on her face.
Her heart, her soul, so full of grace.
She greets everyone with a hug and a kiss.
These happy times we all will miss.
Happy thoughts lived in her mind.
She was always so loving, so caring, so kind.
Now it's time to say goodbye
And let our Nan rest in peace.

Helen Rowberry

SEMPER REFORMANDA

Three hundred years and fifty more will soon have run their course
Since our forefathers in the faith resolved that they perforce
Within the Church Established might no longer fitly stay:
They feared its proud pretensions quite belied the Gospel way.

For them, belonging to Christ's Fold no worldly rôle might be:
Had Christ not told the saints of old, 'Who serve me follow me?'
Those He redeems receive His call to follow in His way;
They know to Him they owe their all, they may not disobey.

These were no pious sectaries with sanctimonious airs,
Rejecting robes and rectories and ritual popish prayers!
They sought to follow where Christ led, according to their lights;
Him only would they own as Head, and His the sole crown rights.

They sought a gathered Church to found, committed to Christ's cause;
By chains that man has made not bound, ruled by no human laws.
How might Christ's Church its task fulfil, in thrall to worldly ways?
How could it do its Master's will, while seeking earthly praise?

In time to come the world may deem these Puritan divines
Had rather too much self-esteem and over-bold designs
When they presumed the Church they knew did not its task fulfil
And sought its nature to renew according to Christ's will.

And yet . . . if we Christ's work would do and not our duty shirk,
We all must constantly review our churches' life and work;
To keep our witness live and warm, to follow in Christ's way,
We must be open to reform - each hour of every day!

Though separation we deplore - it must the world confuse -
The harm done may be even more if we reform refuse.
We, in this great millennial year, remember, by God's grace,
The centuries of faith sincere and witness in this place.

Ronald Manley

GRANNY MAC'S (AN EVOCATION OF LONG AGO)
(To Granny Mac - Memories of whose life and home have been an inspiration ever since)

Behind the house a concrete yard was cool and dark, enclosed,
The southern side, the drive, the flowers, in heat and light reposed.
Three marble steps, an open porch, stained glass beside the door,
Bay windows, and when sirens wailed, a cellar through the floor.
From bedroom's length a balcony that viewed the distant sea,
A wooden garage, rarely used, which stood . . . mysteriously!
Across the road two bungalows, verandas green and cream,
'Calcutta' and 'Bombay' their names - a safe, exotic dream.
Our neighbouring house, its grey-washed side, with intrigue
would enthral,
Mesembryanthemums smiled there atop the wayside wall.
The next-door dwelling slumbered sun-baked, silent and serene,
White alyssum, sweet-scented, grew the paving slabs between.
The following frontage laid to grass had purple salvia wild,
Red roof, red bricks, black beams, white paint, a house mock
Tudor styled.
A bungalow beyond and sudden welcome, open space,
Though drab and bare with spartan lawns, a timeless, peaceful place.
The boundary line a creosote fence - that heady pungent smell,
At sandy base more alyssum, self-seeded, wove its spell.
And last the house within the beach, stone steps to bridge the way,
Its garden coltsfoot gold unkempt, green elder, buckthorn grey.
Brown asphalt formed the avenue - few cars were ever there -
Those squelchy, melting pools of pitch embalmed the quiet air.
How hot along the tarmac path the journey to the shore,
To stand too long brought searing pain brown feet could not ignore.
And then the soft, dry, scorching sand, again too warm to tread,
But underneath to burrowing toes a cooler, damper bed.
Those halcyon hours among the dunes, flags, castles, seagulls' cries,
Idyllic ides of innocence and cloudless summer skies.
How treasured, how evocative those far-off summer days,
Remembered ne'er repeated as the Last Post nearer plays.

Verity Gill Malkinson

A BLINK OF AN EYE
(Dedicated to the late Jean-Donminique Bauby with All My Blinks Of an Eye to Claude Mendibil with all my love for the Masterpiece)

How blind can we all be, for it's here for all of us to see
In a blink of an eye to read from a genius who was in bed but not at ease
He had so many things to say a blink of his eye was his only way
To tell us what he had left, to tell us we had the best, to tell us he lived and loved and won, for his book is published for the public and his children - his number one. Now we the public with our blink of an eye can read the meaning of life as our time goes by. With our blink of an eye we will all see the wonders of life with our love to give and hold that's how it will be.
No diving-bell would hold him for he had the key just like the butterfly he was free. He blinked away with his love to say what we have left at the end of our everyday. God bless my God for my blink of my eye so I can read and see his words in front of me. For when we get down in our troubled time remember this with a blink of an eye you are on the winning side. So if someone winks at you what do you say, 'Wink back I got the message we're number one OK.' From the blink of an eye every new dawn will bring a new era, from a blink of an eye shed no tears for like him we are the victors in all our years, and now the time has come with his blink of his eye to say no more, for he knew we will all see forever.
He is in heaven now, as we all will see with a blink of an eye please blink with me, please blink with me, please blink with me - no end.

David Anton Suessmuth

SUMMER OF LOVE

Your skin so soft like rose petals
and smelling just as sweet.
Pale and fresh, young and new
to me you were a perfect view.
So young and innocent lying there
I long to lay beside you,
to caress your rose petal skin.
But you are far away now
Too far to reach your hand,
the holidays are over, gone
I cry myself to sleep each night
and long to hold you very tight.
I look to the sky and dream of you.
A star shines bright, it did that night
when you and I did promise,
To never leave each other's side
as long as we did live.
But here I am alone again,
where are you my sweet rose
Will I ever see you again?
I pray to God to send me news
of you my darling love.

Ann Boffey

DEDICATION
(Written for Trina - daughter-in-law)

A special person she has to be,
When coming down to reality.
Loving wife and mother too,
Coping with all she has to do.

Making costumes for the show,
Happy faces all aglow.
A cake she made to celebrate,
At the end they all partake.

Apart from that she studies too,
Hoping that she will come through.
Congratulations she has got an A,
It couldn't have been a better day.

Evelyn M Harding

OUR TIMES TOGETHER

F or the times we've spent together, my heart is ever-glad;
R ecalling fondest memories and occasionally - some sad.
I n times of woe and trouble, we often shared our tears;
E ven in our darkest hours, we tried to half our fears.
N ow time is passing us by, and our bodies getting slow;
D eserting things of our youth, our spirits simply grow.
S of if you're feeling sadness, and days they all seem long;
H asten up your gladness, because my shoulders - they're strong.
I f ever we are parted, exploring pastures new, simply
P onder on our friendship, and remember - I'm with you.

Paul Lowe

SEND IT ON AHEAD
(Dedicated to Sir Jimmy Saville who practises what he preaches and 'Sends It On Ahead.')

You cannot take it with you, friend,
You've heard that old cliché
So why not take God at His word
There is no better way.

> Send it on ahead why don't you,
> Send it on ahead.

Now Jesus said before He died
A place I will prepare
That everyone who owns my name
Will come and join me there.

> Send it on ahead why don't you
> Send it on ahead.

He also said don't store up wealth
Your end could be abrupt,
But lay up treasures in heav'n above
Where nothing can corrupt.

> Send it on ahead why don't you
> Send it on ahead

So much depends on how we've lived
Our lives down here on earth
Especially since that day when we
Were given second birth.

> Send it on ahead why don't you
> Send it on ahead.

If we make sure our motive's right
When helping where we can
We may be sure He'll guide us to
Fulfil His Master Plan.

> Send it on ahead why don't you
> Send it on ahead.

Lord Jesus needs those bricks we send
Our's not to reason why
But keep enabling Him to build
Those mansions in the sky.

> Send it on ahead why don't you
> Send it on ahead.

Then when it's time for us to go
And earthly work is done
I pray we'll hear Him speak these words
'Well done, O faithful son'

> Send it on ahead why don't you
> Sent it on ahead.

Keith Johnson

ODE TO MY SISTERS

I remember my dear sisters
and how they took the strain
To help a harassed Mother
and never did complain

Our house was over-crowded
with a family that was large
So it was a continual nightmare
for my mum who was in charge

My sisters did the housework
to keep everything spick and span
As Mother had some paying jobs
to help with her budget plan

It was a struggle and a hardship
with my father ill and old
But with my mum's determination
it kept us from the cold

My mother and my sisters
had a partnership so rare
It kept a hard-up family
from living in despair

Lachlan Taylor

If You Were An Actress

If you were an actress you'd grace the stage
If you were a book I'd read every page
And if I were a house, let us assume
The love in your heart would light every room
If you were the sea I'd never stay dry
Your eyes are the stars in my darkened sky
If the heart has a door you hold the key
Blessed with love and joy you could bring to me.

You're the pot of gold at the rainbow's end
The best of all poetry ever penned
The murmur that comes with each passing breeze
To charm every bird that nests in the trees
To add to the fanfare that heralds spring
You're the greatest love song I'll ever sing
Like the sweet essence of a perfumed mist
Where there in my dreams your lips I have kissed

Your beauty flows on just like a river
Charming the cornfields in swaying quiver
Fulfilling now the promise of May
You're the setting sun at the close of day
And in the night you will still be the queen
Of all that's to come and all that has been
If you were an actress, you'd play the part
Of love's young dream on the stage of my heart.

Albert Edwin Fox

BROKEN LOVE

My heart is a balloon
full of love to be shared,
but nobody loves me
and nobody cares.

If love runs dry
why don't my tears?
Is it because he no longer cares

Let me die and burn away.
He no longer loves me
I've no reason to stay,
and on my tombstone they will write,
her broken heart has taken flight.
Up into the clouds I'll soar,
and there I'll weep forever more.

Kelly Oakley

SUMMER LOVE

The weather was rough
but we didn't care
you'd meet me from work
your brolly we'd share
We'd walk hand in hand
right through the rain
then you'd walk me home
and we'd get wet again
When I had a day off
we'd spend it together
we often thought
it could go on forever
The weather got brighter
we listened to our song
I woke-up one morning
to find you had gone
Now when it rains
I glance at the sky above
in my mind's eye I see us
back in our summer of love.

Joy Benford

LOVE

Where were you when I needed your love,
Your help, your strength, your warmth?
When I needed you the most, you were gone.

Gone from sight, touch, heart.
I hated you for leaving me,
Alone, in the cold and darkness.
It surrounded me.

The loneliness surrounded me.
I was trapped and hurt.
An unloved soul in a wicked world - and you laughed.
It echoed in my ears and all around.
I could hear you . . . laughing.

I screamed . . . you dare laugh at me?
In my time of need you'd taken away my independence
And now taken away my love.
I had dared to believe in you - even depend on you.

You had destroyed me, deserted me, taken away my life.
But thou shalt not shed a tear
Thou shalt shed a hundred tears.

An emptiness had grown within me, I was weak and ill.
One day I didn't wake-up. Not in this world, but in another.

A light shone, it drew me towards it.
I could see happiness beyond.
But then your voice. It came and warned me!
I fled away from the light. I awoke in a hospital room.
You were there. I had touched death. You had saved me!

When I thought I had needed you the most, I hadn't.
You came when I was on the edge of my life.
You stopped me leaping and saved my soul.
My emptiness was filled. You are my life. I love you.

Virginia Withers

Is This Really Goodbye

Time was when we were young lovers, our thoughts of only each other
Plans and high hopes of a brilliant future together
Each day dawned in eager anticipation of each other's touch
Of tenderness, kisses and longing for the day we were to be married
So much love, so much care, so much devotion
Each minute apart was as an hour, each hour together as a minute
Our young lives seemed to pass as a fleeting moment

Time came when we were married, joined as one together, a new chapter
Looking forward to building our own home, a new adventure
Together our love was forged with the gift of children, the fruits of our love
Daily parenting became a learning experience no blueprints to guide us
Our happy children nurtured, loved, guided into young adults
So proud we watched as they fled the nest to build a life of their own
Stepping out to take young lovers of their own
To grow and experience life's trials and tribulations

Time has come and alone we are once more
Our bustling happy home silent, echoes of laughter fill the empty rooms
Quarrels are now a part of our once planned brilliant future
Life has taken its toll, what expectations are left
Together the company of one another is no longer enough
How did things go so wrong, did we neglect each other along the way
What happened to the young lovers of long ago, the aspirations the plans
How did we stumble, how did we drift apart, when did we stop caring
Can we learn to love one another all over again
Or has time eaten away at the true feelings we had, the love we shared
Can we rekindle our young love and carry it on into the twilight years
Or is this really goodbye!

Carolyn Foggin

THOUGHTS

I lay on my back on the summer grass
And looked up at the blue, blue sky;
Warmed by the sun, and lulled
By the buzz of a pollen'd bee, close by.
The apple blossom, tinged with pink,
And pear buds, reached for the sky,
And I thought of you, no longer here -
Yet your spirit comes close by.

Then a blackbird sang of the English spring
And of new life coming to birth,
And I thought how all your loving care
Gave me your love of our earth.

Mary Dimond

To My Sister-In-Law

It's such a pleasure this day to greet,
A sister-in-law, kind, thoughtful and sweet.
'Happy Birthday' and best wishes to you I send,
May this be a memorable day from beginning to end.

To mark this occasion I have no diamonds or gold,
But the presents I bring you are more precious to hold,
Sincere love and affection are the gifts I bring to you,
Not only for this day, but for all your life through.

If I could grant wishes and make them come true,
I'd wish away all the pain suffered by you,
But I have no power to grant wishes you see,
Only God knows what is best for you and for me.

May God's love surround you every hour of each day,
Just take His hand, He will guide your way,
Life here on earth is a probation you see,
Assessing our worth, that we might inherit, Life Eternally.

Muriel Schönfield

A Life To Lose
(Dedicated to my son Ieuan)

A lot to lose,
Too much to lose,
Life to lose,
Hold on tightly and don't let go;
'Cause I gotta lot to lose,
Too much to lose,
A life to lose.
I thought I saw the light,
Did you see the light?
It shone through my window;
And picked a spot in the corner to rest upon,
It showed me the way forward,
The future,
It reminded me;
To hold-on tight and never let go,
'Cause I've got too much to lose,
A life to lose.

***Barry Holland**

Love At First Sight

I loved her since that first glance
And knew there'd be a time for us
A seedling borne on the wind of chance
I have it here within me
A tender note of music with impending symphony.
I guard it as if it were a child
Less my passion may suppress
This growing flower of my love
My all my very happiness.
Her dream has been with me all day
Now into my warm and drowsy night
That sunny hope draws closer
Into the shadows of my solitude
And as I sit in thought and stare
Out where the great lights meet the city glare.
Happy to sleep knowing she is out there somewhere
God make a time for us is my only prayer

Brian McDoneli

MY SUMMER LOVE

Spring alerted and directed my gaze into his direction,
I told myself: 'Be patient, wait, don't hurry - lest there is rejection -
If his heart you wish to win, plan things and make your move in
    glorious summer.'
I obeyed my instincts, worked on my plans and when tired rested
    dreamt sweet dreams in my slumber.

A summer of love I had planned, hoped, prayed and longed for;
I had dreamt that my love for him would open his love closed door -
The sweet smell of nectar had enticed the busy honey bees to the
    beautiful coloured petals of my garden
How I wished that he would tread a path to the door of this
    love-struck maiden.

Then one bright July evening he paused, then stopped and walked
    towards my front door;
My happy heart skipped a beat - I couldn't have wished for more -
Just a visit from this tall, vibrant stranger would be enough for me,
'Hello!' he said, 'My name is Jonah, may I invite myself in for tea?'

'Well, I don't know, this sort of thing is not done around here -
I don't know you,' I sighed, 'But many a time have seen you harmlessly
    passing going everywhere.'
'I won't harm you,' said he, 'I live six houses away at number
    sixty-one -
And if you don't believe me - here's my card - I hope you can fit me
    into your little plan.'

'My little plan? -What can he mean - can he really read my mind?'
'Oh, do come inside.' - To have said anything else would have been
    so unkind.
He made himself at home; home from home only six houses away
He had that resigned and contented look that shouted, 'I've really come
    here to stay!'

Soon we became inseparable and decided to tie the knot,
A year later this new Mrs was nursing baby Clara in a brightly coloured
    pink cot -
That summer of love had paved the way to a happy life for Jonah and I
And I bless the day that I opened the door to him, braving my heart's
    reticence although I've always been so shy.

Margaret Andrews

Today I Saw An Angel

Today I saw an angel,
Sitting on the step beneath me,
No wings, no smile, no halo,
Just sadness,
I asked her what was wrong,
She turned to reply, and spoke in the
Sweetest voice, I have ever heard.
For some reason, she had lost her smile,
I asked her how that could happen
She said something,
I could not hear her,
She was no longer with me,
But I was left,
With a smile in my heart.

Leah Danielle Carey

To My Beautiful And Precious Niece, Lauren

I bless the day that she was born
My niece, she's six, her name is Lauren
She's brought us laughter and so much joy
Even though she acts just like a boy!
I love it when she stays with me
'Cause I don't have any kids you see
So every Friday it means so much
To get her cuddles and feel her touch
Sometimes we paint, or bake, or sing
Or dance and laugh, and do crazy things!
But we always make sure we have lots of fun
And on Saturdays she hopes for sun
'Cause it means her football shorts go on
And she can run about singing football songs
To watch her now, you'd never tell
That last year she was very ill
She's getting better and has put on weight
To see her healthy is just so great
Last year, she also started school
Though she was sick a lot, she's nobody's fool
The speed at which she can read and write
Has been keeping me up each week, all night
To read 'The Wishing Chair' and 'The Faraway Tree'
I can't skip words now she can read, you see!
She can even add up and take-away
And use a computer mouse, it's essential these days
She won a CD hi-fi for her colouring-in
And I think she's so cute with a cheeky wee grin
No money in this world will ever measure up
To my title of 'Auntie' and my niece's love.

'Auntie' Lynn Harper

Mother

To you who read these lines
Tender words I want to say
Remember Mother gave you *life*
Happy, happy day.

From babyhood to growing-up
With hazards on your way
You have managed to do much
We all grow older every day.

You came with 'lasting-love-forever'
Make sure Mum know you care
To her your kindness means so much
Don't leave her unaware.

As life is full of changes
Days may come when you are sad
Mother being gone forever
Then you might wish you had
        said 'Mother, I love you.'

Marion Warby

It Had To Happen

We were in love for many years
We got wed on the day we met
Yet years have gone past
I thought it would last
It had to happen
We parted with tears
It had to happen
Why, I did not know
We both cried
I did not want to go
Can we try again?
What went wrong?
It had to happen
We were not that strong
After all the years
We loved each other so
Yes it had to happen,
Now I must go.

P M Wardle

THOUGHTS OF YOU

Your face, your voice, your everything,
Has filled me with desire.
This chemistry, this feeling,
Like gentle flames of fire.

You captivated my heart.
Why - I can't explain,
I know you're out of reach,
Your love I cannot claim.

Those friendly eyes - boyish smile,
The caring work you do.
You see it has been easy -
To fall in love with you.

My heart saw a person with qualities,
I'd choose for my very own,
But I don't think I'll feel the same again
Alas! I'll be left on my own.

My heart sinks sadly when I think of you,
Knowing things cannot be,
For you are in an authoritative position
And couldn't fall for me.

Nevertheless I fell for you,
These thoughts I shouldn't feel.
You already have a love,
Your heart I shall not steal.

So you will remain just a pleasant dream,
An obsession I think you'd say,
I shall think of you for a moment or so,
Then brush the thought away.

Wendy Watkin

Sun On My Face

The sun on my face
And the wind in my hair
Walks on the beach
Days at the fair

His eyes sent a message
His hands gave a sign
I knew what I wanted
He had to be mine

The way that he touched me
Made my heart skip a beat
Goose pimples appeared
From my head to my feet

I made him my soulmate
The dream wouldn't last
Without conscious thought
It happened so fast

The days they flew by
Weeks, only two
Sun on my face
Reminds me of you.

Zoe Westwood

YOU GAVE ME LOVE

I was trapped like a bird,
    but no-one listened
      'Until You heard'.
In the darkness of the night,
'You answered to my plight'.
You set me free from
    all the pain
      inside of me.
You reached out from above
'Showering me with love'.
Like the stillness of the sea,
'Your calmness
    washing over me.'
No longer lonely and
    tormented inside,
'Now I have You Lord
    as my Guide.

Janet 'Rose' Marsh

TO MY LOVER

It would be easy to say goodbye to you, right away
Tomorrow will come to take my thoughts away
I could drift back and swallow tears
of my married life
of all these years.
> But life would be without a spark
> my life has changed
> You've left your mark for all to see
> that I'm not me
> no longer the woman I used to be.

But if at night, at home,
I lie alone,
will I be strong or will I cry for Tom?
For I don't know what the future holds
for you and me
in eternity.
Maybe that's it, it's bye for now
I'll just go back, I don't want your spark.
It burns too hot, your fire is too much
it melts my brain, I cannot see
it burns my thoughts
it melts me low
please say goodbye to me.

But, if you do and if we part,
my life will be without a spark
my life has changed
you've left your mark
for all to see
that I'm not me
no longer the woman I used to be.

Marcela Griffiths

THE LOVE OF MY LIFE

He left me with
A broken heart,
Which he himself
Had torn apart.

We once had some love
Which we both shared,
He used to tell me
That he cared.

I wander around my house
Feeling so insane,
But wishing that
I could see him again.

Just to find out
What I'm supposed to have done,
And why I seem
To feel so numb.

We used to be so happy
But that has certainly changed,
Now he's gone for good
My life's been rearranged.

Laura Keightley (16)

LOVE

We have to let go
There's nothing to show.
Love is like waves on the shore -
No ripples for us anymore.
My feelings I'm trying to hide -
Love has to flow with the tide
It ebbs and we go our own ways
You're gone and I'm left in a daze
Love is rough and it's smooth
Now there's no one to soothe.

Ann Dutschak

INFORMATION

We hope you have enjoyed reading this book - and that you will continue to enjoy it in the coming years.

If you like reading and writing poetry drop us a line, or give us a call, and we'll send you a free information pack.

Write to :-
**Triumph House Information
1-2 Wainman Road
Woodston
Peterborough
PE2 7BU
(01733) 230749**